APR 1 3 2009

Protect Our Planet

Global Warming

Angela Royston

Heinemann Library
Chicago, IL

© 2008 Heinemann Library
a division of Reed Elsevier Inc.

Customer Service **888-454-2279**

Design: Joanna Hinton-Malivoire
Picture research: Melissa Allison, Fiona Orbell and Erica Martin
Production: Duncan Gilbert
Printed and bound in China by South China Printing Co. Ltd.

12 11 10 09 08
10 9 8 7 6 5 4 3 2

10-digit ISBN: 1-4329-0924-X (hc)
                 1-4329-0930-4 (pb)

Library of Congress Cataloging-in-Publication Data

Royston, Angela.
  Global warming / Angela Royston.
    p. cm. -- (Protect our planet)
  Includes bibliographical references and index.
  ISBN-13: 978-1-4329-0924-6 (hc)
  ISBN-13: 978-1-4329-0930-7 (pb)
  1. Global warming--Juvenile literature. I. Title.
  QC981.8.G56R69 2008
  363.738'74--dc22
                    2007043911

Acknowledgements
The publishers would like to thank the following for permission to reproduce photographs: © Alamy p.**12** (Medio Images); © Corbis RF p.**21**; © Digital Stock p.**19**; © Digital Vision p.**17**; © Ecoscene p.**25 right** (Eva Miessler); © Getty Images pp.**13** (AFP), **4**, **16** (Photodisc); © NaturePL p.**27** (Arco Reinhard); © Panos pp.**9** (Alex Smalles), **8** (Dieter Telemans), **28** (Jocelyn Carlin), **11** (Karen Robinson); © Pearson Education Ltd p.**25 left** (Gareth Boden); © Photolibrary pp.**5** (Daniel Morrison), **14** (Josephine Schiele), **24** (Spence Inqa); © Punchstock p.**20** (Fancy); © REUTERS p.**29** (Fabrizio Bensch); © Science Photo Library p.**7** (Simon Fraser); © Still Pictures pp.**22** (Hardy Haenel), **18** (Hartmut Schwarzbach, argus), **23** (Jochen Tack, Das Fotoarchiv), **26** (Martin Bond)

Cover photograph of melting icebergs reproduced with permission of © Corbis (Paul Souders).

Every effort has been made to contact copyright holders of any material reproduced in this book. Any omissions will be rectified in subsequent printings if notice is given to the publishers.

Contents

Some words are shown in bold, **like this**. You can find out what they mean by looking in the Glossary.

What Is the Earth?

The Earth is one of the **planets** that circles around the Sun. The Earth has land, oceans, rivers, and air. It is the only planet where scientists know for sure that living things exist.

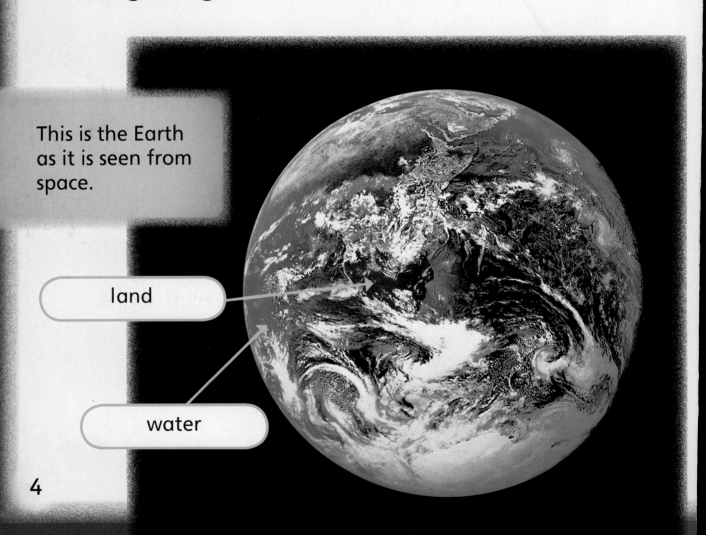

This is the Earth as it is seen from space.

land

water

The Sun shines on the Earth and gives it light and heat. The Earth gets the right amount of heat for millions of different plants and animals to live here.

What Is Global Warming?

The temperature of the Earth has risen a small amount during the last 100 years. This is called **global warming**.

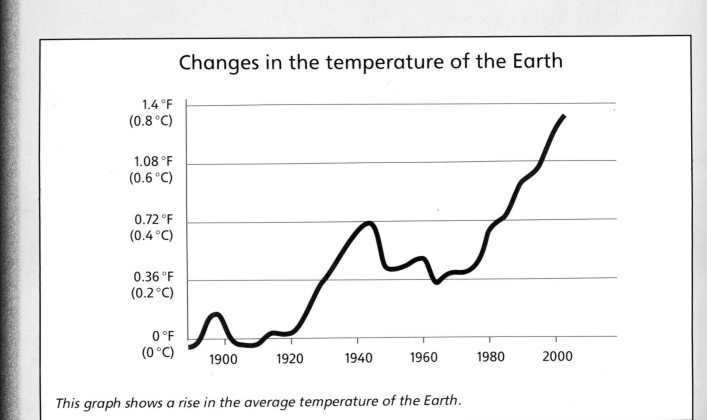

Changes in the temperature of the Earth

This graph shows a rise in the average temperature of the Earth.

Most of the rise in the temperature of the Earth has happened in the last few years.

This is a weather thermometer. It measures the temperature of the air.

Some parts of the Earth are always hotter or colder than other parts. Global warming is making most places on the Earth a little warmer.

More Extreme Weather

Global warming is changing the weather in many areas of the world. In some places the summer is now hotter than it used to be. And in many places it rains much less than it used to.

This dry land used to be a golf course. It was covered with grass.

KEEP OFF GRASS

Strong winds can damage buildings and cause flooding.

Hurricanes are storms with very strong winds. In some places hurricanes are getting stronger.

Bigger Deserts

Deserts are places that get almost no rain. Very few plants, animals, or people can live in a desert. **Global warming** is making deserts larger.

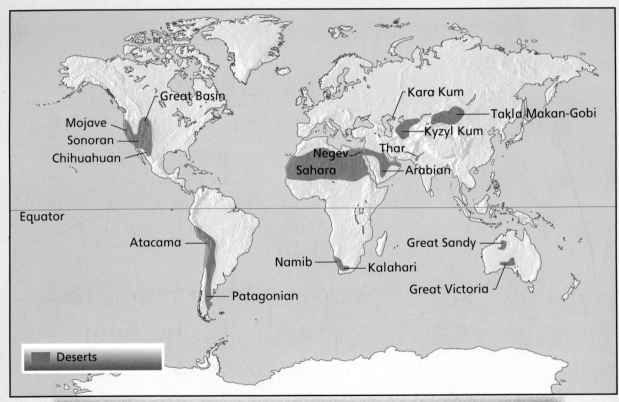

Great Basin

Mojave
Sonoran
Chihuahuan

Kara Kum

Takla Makan-Gobi

Kyzyl Kum

Thar

Negev
Sahara

Arabian

Equator

Atacama

Namib

Kalahari

Great Sandy

Great Victoria

Patagonian

Deserts

The world's deserts are shown here in yellow. Global warming is causing more land to become desert.

This land in the country Kenya is becoming too dry for these goats to live on.

More land is becoming too dry for plants to grow. When this happens, there is nothing for animals to eat. The people who live on the land have to move somewhere else.

Melting Ice

The **Arctic** and **Antarctic** are the coldest parts of the Earth. They are covered with very thick ice all year. **Global warming** is causing some of this ice to melt.

If the temperature of the Earth continues to rise, more and more cities will be flooded.

As the ice melts, extra water runs into the oceans. This means that the level of the sea is slowly rising. If the sea rises too much, it will flood cities, towns, and land near the coast.

What Causes Global Warming?

The air is a mixture of gases. One of the gases is **carbon dioxide**. Carbon dioxide and some other gases in the air are called **greenhouse gases**.

A greenhouse is warm inside because it traps the Sun's heat.

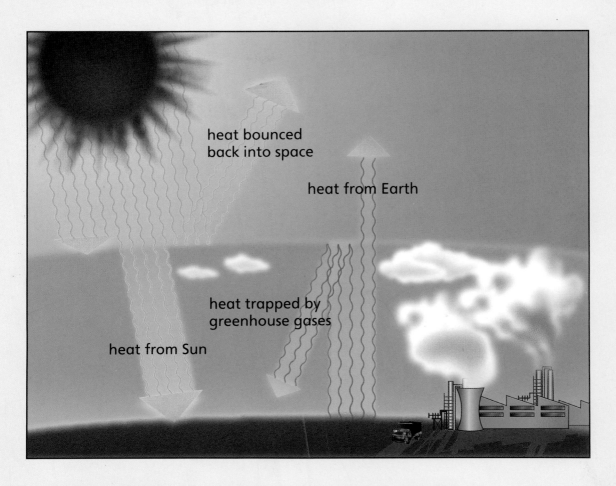

heat bounced
back into space

heat from Earth

heat trapped by
greenhouse gases

heat from Sun

Greenhouse gases trap some of the
Sun's heat. The amount of carbon
dioxide and other greenhouses gases in
the air is increasing. This is causing the
Earth to become warmer.

Where Does Carbon Dioxide Come From?

Global warming is caused by extra **carbon dioxide** in the air. Almost all of this extra carbon dioxide is made by people when they burn **oil**, coal, and **natural gas**.

Most cars burn gasoline to work. When gasoline burns, it makes carbon dioxide.

This power station burns coal to make electricity.

People use oil to make **fuel** for cars, trucks, and airplanes. **Power stations** burn coal, oil, and natural gas to make **electricity**. People use electricity to light buildings and to make televisions and other machines work.

Can Global Warming Be Stopped?

People can slow down **global warming** by burning less coal, **oil**, and **natural gas**. Scientists are inventing new **fuels** and engines that do not make as much **carbon dioxide**. These are called **low-carbon** fuels and engines.

This bus uses a fuel that makes no carbon dioxide.

Wind turbines make electricity when their blades turn in the wind.

Scientists have invented ways of making **electricity** without burning coal, oil, and natural gas. One way is to use the power of the wind. **Wind turbines** can make electricity. They do not create carbon dioxide.

Low-Carbon Electricity

Some **power stations** use moving water to make **electricity**. A **dam** is built across a valley to make a lake. Some of the water from the lake flows through the dam and the power station. This kind of power station does not make **carbon dioxide**.

dam

This power station uses water to make electricity.

This power station uses the heat of the Sun's rays to make electricity.

The Sun can be used to make electricity. Many mirrors guide the Sun's rays onto one spot. Here a liquid becomes very hot. The heat is used to make electricity.

Low-Carbon Homes

Scientists are finding ways to make buildings **low-carbon**. Some buildings have solar panels on their roofs. These use sunlight to make **electricity** and do not make **carbon dioxide**. They work during the day but not at night.

solar panels

regular light bulb

low-energy light bulbs

Homes can be designed so they use less electricity or natural gas for heating and cooling. People can also save energy by using low-energy light bulbs.

The Bigger Picture

Carbon dioxide created in one part of the world causes **global warming** all around the world. The United States and China make the most carbon dioxide.

Tuvalu is an island in the South Pacific. It is becoming flooded because of global warming.

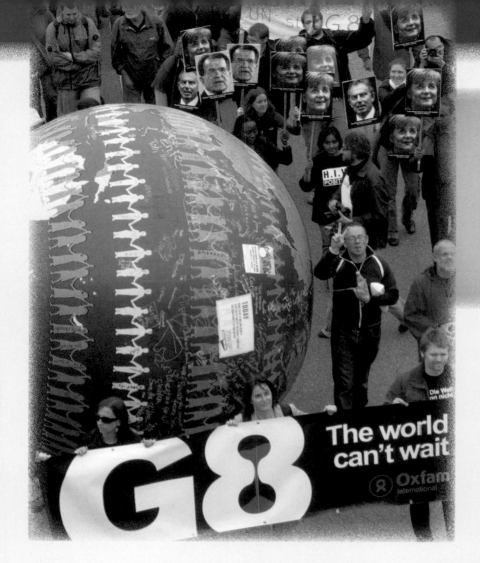

These people want countries to agree to cut the amount of carbon dioxide they create.

All countries need to work together to cut the amount of carbon dioxide they are creating. If they do so, they can help to stop the worst problems of global warming.

Glossary

Antarctic land and sea around the South Pole where it is very cold all year round

Arctic land and ocean around the North Pole where it is very cold all year round

biofuel fuel made from plants that vehicles can use to make them move

carbon dioxide one of the gases in the air. Carbon dioxide is a greenhouse gas.

dam wall that blocks a river to make a lake

desert area of dry land that gets very little rain

electricity form of energy used to make machines work

electric motor engine that uses electricity to make something work

fuel substance such as gas, wood, or coal that is burned to give heat, light, or power

global warming rise in temperature of the surface of the Earth, including the land, sea, and air

greenhouse gas gas in the air that traps some of the Sun's heat and makes the Earth warmer

low-carbon making very little or no carbon dioxide

natural gas gas that is found under the ground. It is burned in homes to make heat.

oil liquid found under the ground. It is burned in vehicles and in power stations.

planet huge lump of rock or a large mass of gas and liquid that circles around a star

power station building where electricity is made

wind turbine machine that makes electricity using blades that spin in the wind

Find Out More

Books to read

Fix, Alexandra. *Energy*. Chicago: Heinemann Library, 2007.

Rockwell, Anne and Paul Meisel. *Why Are the Ice Caps Melting?*. New York: HarperCollins, 2006.

Websites to visit

www.epa.gov/climatechange/kids/
This is the website of the United States Environmental Protection Agency. It gives information about global warming.

tiki.oneworld.net/global-warming/climate-home.html
Tiki the penguin tells you how global warming is affecting his home.

Index